PRINCE
HALL

4-19-92

Dear Marty,

To a prince of a pearl,

All best,

Arthur (JD) Diamond

PRINCE HALL

Arthur Diamond

Senior Consulting Editor
Nathan Irvin Huggins
Director
W.E.B. Du Bois Institute for Afro-American Research
Harvard University

CHELSEA HOUSE PUBLISHERS
New York   Philadelphia

To the memory of Charles and Thelma Diamond

Chelsea House Publishers
Editor-in-Chief Remmel Nunn
Managing Editor Karyn Gullen Browne
Copy Chief Mark Rifkin
Picture Editor Adrian G. Allen
Art Director Maria Epes
Assistant Art Director Noreen Romano
Manufacturing Director Gerald Levine
Systems Manager Lindsey Ottman
Production Manager Joseph Romano
Production Coordinator Marie Claire Cebrián

Black Americans of Achievement
Senior Editor Richard Rennert

Staff for PRINCE HALL
Copy Editor Christopher Duffy
Editorial Assistant Michele Haddad
Picture Researcher Nisa Rauschenberg
Designer Ghila Krajzman
Cover Illustration William Giese

First Printing

1 3 5 7 9 8 6 4 2

Library of Congress Cataloging-in-Publication Data
Diamond, Arthur.
    Prince Hall: social reformer/by Arthur Diamond.
        p.   cm.—(Black Americans of achievement)
    Includes bibliographical references and index.
    Summary: A summary of the life and career of the black social
reformer.
    ISBN 1-55546-588-9
        0-7910-0239-X (pbk.)
    1. Hall, Prince, 1735–1807—Juvenile literature.   2. Afro-
Americans—Biography—Juvenile literature.   3. Afro-American
freemasons—Biography—Juvenile literature.   4. Freemasons—
United States—Biography—Juvenile literature.   [1. Hall,
Prince, 1735–1807.   2. Freemasons.   3. Afro-Americans—
Biography.]   I. Title.   II. Series.
E185.97.H25D53   1991   91-13424
366′.1′092—dc20   CIP
[B]   AC

Frontispiece: *A view of Boston
Harbor as it appeared in the 18th
century.*

CONTENTS

BLACK AMERICANS OF ACHIEVEMENT

RALPH ABERNATHY
civil rights leader

MUHAMMAD ALI
heavyweight champion

RICHARD ALLEN
religious leader and social activist

LOUIS ARMSTRONG
musician

ARTHUR ASHE
tennis great

JOSEPHINE BAKER
entertainer

JAMES BALDWIN
author

BENJAMIN BANNEKER
scientist and mathematician

AMIRI BARAKA
poet and playwright

COUNT BASIE
bandleader and composer

ROMARE BEARDEN
artist

JAMES BECKWOURTH
frontiersman

MARY MCLEOD BETHUNE
educator

BLANCHE BRUCE
politician

RALPH BUNCHE
diplomat

GEORGE WASHINGTON CARVER
botanist

CHARLES CHESNUTT
author

BILL COSBY
entertainer

PAUL CUFFE
merchant and abolitionist

FATHER DIVINE
religious leader

FREDERICK DOUGLASS
abolitionist editor

CHARLES DREW
physician

W.E.B. DU BOIS
scholar and activist

PAUL LAURENCE DUNBAR
poet

KATHERINE DUNHAM
dancer and choreographer

MARIAN WRIGHT EDELMAN
civil rights leader and lawyer

DUKE ELLINGTON
bandleader and composer

RALPH ELLISON
author

JULIUS ERVING
basketball great

JAMES FARMER
civil rights leader

ELLA FITZGERALD
singer

MARCUS GARVEY
black-nationalist leader

DIZZY GILLESPIE
musician

PRINCE HALL
social reformer

W. C. HANDY
father of the blues

WILLIAM HASTIE
educator and politician

MATTHEW HENSON
explorer

CHESTER HIMES
author

BILLIE HOLIDAY
singer

JOHN HOPE
educator

LENA HORNE
entertainer

LANGSTON HUGHES
poet

ZORA NEALE HURSTON
author

JESSE JACKSON
civil rights leader and politician

JACK JOHNSON
heavyweight champion

JAMES WELDON JOHNSON
author

SCOTT JOPLIN
composer

BARBARA JORDAN
politician

MARTIN LUTHER KING, JR.
civil rights leader

ALAIN LOCKE
scholar and educator

JOE LOUIS
heavyweight champion

RONALD MCNAIR
astronaut

MALCOLM X
militant black leader

THURGOOD MARSHALL
Supreme Court justice

ELIJAH MUHAMMAD
religious leader

JESSE OWENS
champion athlete

CHARLIE PARKER
musician

GORDON PARKS
photographer

SIDNEY POITIER
actor

ADAM CLAYTON POWELL, JR.
political leader

LEONTYNE PRICE
opera singer

A. PHILIP RANDOLPH
labor leader

PAUL ROBESON
singer and actor

JACKIE ROBINSON
baseball great

BILL RUSSELL
basketball great

JOHN RUSSWURM
publisher

SOJOURNER TRUTH
antislavery activist

HARRIET TUBMAN
antislavery activist

NAT TURNER
slave revolt leader

DENMARK VESEY
slave revolt leader

MADAM C. J. WALKER
entrepreneur

BOOKER T. WASHINGTON
educator

HAROLD WASHINGTON
politician

WALTER WHITE
civil rights leader and author

RICHARD WRIGHT
author

ON
ACHIEVEMENT

———— ❧ ————

Coretta Scott King

Bᴇғᴏʀᴇ ʏᴏᴜ ʙᴇɢɪɴ this book, I hope you will ask yourself what the word excellence means to you. I think that it's a question we should all ask, and keep asking as we grow older and change. Because the truest answer to it should never change. When you think of excellence, perhaps you think of success at work; or of becoming wealthy; or meeting the right person, getting married, and having a good family life.

Those important goals are worth striving for, but there is a better way to look at excellence. As Martin Luther King, Jr., said in one of his last sermons, "I want you to be first in love. I want you to be first in moral excellence. I want you to be first in generosity. If you want to be important, wonderful. If you want to be great, wonderful. But recognize that he who is greatest among you shall be your servant."

My husband, Martin Luther King, Jr., knew that the true meaning of achievement is service. When I met him, in 1952, he was already ordained as a Baptist preacher and was working towards a doctoral degree at Boston University. I was studying at the New England Conservatory and dreamed of accomplishments in music. We married a year later, and after I graduated the following year we moved to Montgomery, Alabama. We didn't know it then, but our notions of achievement were about to undergo a dramatic change.

You may have read or heard about what happened next. What began with the boycott of a local bus line grew into a national movement, and by the time he was assassinated in 1968 my husband had fashioned a black movement powerful enough to shatter forever the practice of racial segregation. What you may not have read about is where he got his method for resisting injustice without compromising his religious beliefs.

He adopted the strategy of nonviolence from a man of a different race, who lived in a distant country, and even practiced a different religion. The man was Mahatma Gandhi, the great leader of India, who devoted his life to serving humanity in the spirit of love and nonviolence. It was in these principles that Martin discovered his method for social reform. More than anything else, those two principles were the key to his achievements.

This book is about black Americans who served society through the excellence of their achievements. It forms a part of the rich history of black men and women in America—a history of stunning accomplishments in every field of human endeavor, from literature and art to science, industry, education, diplomacy, athletics, jurisprudence, even polar exploration.

Not all of the people in this history had the same ideals, but I think you will find something that all of them have in common. Like Martin Luther King, Jr., they all decided to become "drum majors" and serve humanity. In that principle—whether it was expressed in books, inventions, or song—they found something outside themselves to use as a goal and a guide. Something that showed them a way to serve others, instead of living only for themselves.

Reading the stories of these courageous men and women not only helps us discover the principles that we will use to guide our own lives but also teaches us about our black heritage and about America itself. It is crucial for us to know the heroes and heroines of our history and to realize that the price we paid in our struggle for equality in America was dear. But we must also understand that we have gotten as far as we have partly because America's democratic system and ideals made it possible.

We are still struggling with racism and prejudice. But the great men and women in this series are a tribute to the spirit of our democratic ideals and the system in which they have flourished. And that makes their stories special and worth knowing.

PRINCE
HALL

———◆———

1

"A MAN OF BENEVOLENCE AND CHARITY"

—❦—

ON THE EVENING of March 6, 1775—just a month before the start of the American Revolution— Prince Hall led a group of 14 black colonists through the muddy streets of Boston toward the area known as Bunker Hill. The city was quiet, but the silence was misleading. Boston was filled with tension over the upcoming war.

A typically unsettling brush between the local colonists and British troops had taken place the previous night at Boston's Old South Church. There, Dr. Joseph Warren, a leading advocate in the anti-British movement, prepared to give a speech honoring the fifth anniversary of the Boston Massacre, a small skirmish that had claimed the lives of five procolonist rioters. Samuel Adams, John Hancock, and Dr. Benjamin Rush were among the prominent American patriots who had gathered to hear Warren speak.

Prince Hall was perhaps the most highly respected free black in Boston around the time of the American Revolution. He was the founder of the first black Masonic order and an outspoken opponent of slavery.

Just as the physician was about to utter his first words, more than three dozen British soldiers entered the church. The redcoats' purpose, the audience knew, was to listen carefully to Warren. If he said anything the soldiers considered dangerous to the British cause, then they would arrest him in full view of his friends and supporters.

Warren proceeded to speak calmly, in measured tones, about some of the problems that the colonists were facing under British rule. Yet at no time did he incite the audience. As a result, the redcoats did not have any cause to arrest him.

As soon as Warren concluded his speech, however, word flashed through the church that someone had set fire to the building. Soldiers and patriots rushed out of their seats and into the street—just in time to meet another unit of redcoats marching by. Fearing that these troops might think a riot had broken out in the church and decide to take action against the colonists, Warren explained firmly to the British soldiers about the fire. (As it turned out, the rumor had been false.)

Warren was able to keep anyone from being seriously harmed, but he could not prevent a small scuffle from breaking out between the redcoats and a few of the American patriots. With the city on the brink of war, everyone was on edge.

Well aware of the tense atmosphere, Prince Hall made sure to choose a route through the back streets as he guided his small band through Boston the next evening. While skirting the garrisons and roadblocks set up by the British, the group also watched out for squads of colonial vigilantes. Hall and his companions knew that both the colonists and the British had been competing for the allegiance of free blacks; accordingly, each side viewed Hall's party as possible enemies as well as potential friends.

Hall, for one, had openly voiced his displeasure with the British. And yet his life in the American colonies had been far from perfect. The 40-year-old Hall had spent most of it as a slave. He had been granted his freedom only 5 years earlier, when his master, William Hall, decided to manumit (release from slavery) him after 21 years of faithful service.

Prince Hall's circumstances did not improve radically when he was released from slavery. In colonial times, blacks who were granted their liberty still had their life governed by strict legal codes, just as when they had been slaves. These so-called black codes required them to remain in their own neighborhood and, in most cases, ordered them off the streets by 9:00 P.M. Any free black caught outside after that hour risked being arrested and flogged.

Prince Hall refused to be intimidated, however. He was convinced his race could improve its lot in the 13 American colonies if his people became organized. The way colonial society was set up, though, it was impossible for blacks to establish their own organization. The only way they could form any sort of movement to promote the welfare of blacks was through an already existing network.

Hall knew of just such a society: the Fraternal Order of the Free and Accepted Masons. By the late 18th century, the Masons had already formed the world's largest private society. It had originated during medieval times, most likely out of a stonemasons guild, an association of builders. (Even today, few specifics about the Masons are known to nonmembers because information about the society is kept secret by its members.)

The chief purpose of Freemasonry, as one member put it in 1735, "is to be a Man of Benevolence and Charity, not sitting down contented while his Fellow Creatures, but much more his Brethren, are in Want,

BOSTON

when it is in his Power (without prejudicing himself or Family) to relieve them." In order to become a Mason, a person must be willing to promote these ideals of friendship and brotherhood. Moreover, wrote another member in 1738, a Mason "is oblig'd, by his Tenure, . . . to that Religion in which all Men agree, leaving their particular Opinions to themselves; that is, to be *good* Men *and true*, or Men of

RLES TOWN

In the early stages of the American Revolution, the June 17, 1775, Battle of Bunker Hill was a costly victory for the British, who won this encounter but lost 1,054 men while the Americans lost 441. The battle greatly encouraged the colonists because of the heavy casualties they inflicted on the British.

Honour and Honesty." Although Freemasonry is not a religious organization, a Mason believes in only one God and maintains that the best way to worship Him is through service to others.

Hall was convinced that Freemasonry's history of working toward the betterment of man made the society an ideal organization to advance the cause of black equality. Yet most Masons in the colonies did

Major General Thomas Gage, the governor of Massachusetts and commander of the British forces in the American colonies, closed all British military sites to the colonists in 1775. Hall and 14 companions, however, were admitted into British Army Lodge No. 441, where they were initiated into the Masonic order.

not agree with this view. Each time Hall attempted to join Masonic lodges headed by colonists in the Boston area, his bid for membership was turned down. Even though these Masons preached brotherhood, they insisted on keeping blacks out of their lodges.

After being rejected by the colonists' lodges, Hall felt he had little choice but to turn to the British Masons. He sided with the colonies in their growing quest for freedom from British rule, yet he was uncertain that blacks would be granted equal rights if the colonies were successful in severing their ties with Mother England.

Perhaps eager to divide the colonies any way they could, the British Masons offered to initiate Hall and his friends into the society. And so, on the evening of March 6, Hall's party hastened through the streets of Boston toward British Army Lodge No. 441, where the British Masons were stationed. Major General Thomas Gage, the governor of Massachusetts and the commander of the British forces in the American colonies, had closed the lodge to all colonists, as he had every other British military site. But when Hall and the others arrived there, John Batt, a sergeant in the 38th Foot Regiment, warmly greeted them, then locked the door after they had stepped inside.

A significant moment in American history was about to take place. Prince Hall and his 14 companions—Peter Best, Duff Buform, John Canton, Peter Freeman, Fortin Howard, Cyrus Johnbus, Prince Payden, Prince Rees, Thomas Sanderson, Bueston Slinger, Cato Speain, Boston Smith, Benjamin Tiber, and Richard Tilley—were taking the initial steps to form America's first black institution. Inside the lodge, they paid a small sum for the right to be initiated into the Fraternal Order of the Free and Accepted Masons.

To this day, the initiation rites of Freemasonry are supposed to be known only to Masons, for they have sworn never to discuss them. Nevertheless, a few details about Masonic ceremonies have leaked out over the centuries.

One of these accounts, from the 18th century, suggests that during Prince Hall's lifetime, the first part of the initiation ceremony consisted of threats of violence that were meant to frighten the newcomers into following the rules of Freemasonry. Warned that the lodge would punish them if they revealed the society's secrets to outsiders, every initiate was ordered to repeat at the ceremony:

> Here come I the youngest and last entered apprentice. As I am sworn by God and Saint John, by the square and compass and common judge to attend my master's service at the honorable lodge, from Monday in the morning till Saturday at night, and to keep the keys therof, under no less pain than having my tongue cut out under my chin and of being buried within the flood mark where no man shall know.

Each initiate was then told to draw his fingers across his throat to indicate the fate that awaited him if he broke the Masonic rules. After this part of the ceremony was finished, he heard the following pronouncement:

> By God Himself and as you shall answer to God when you shall stand naked before Him, at the great day, you shall not reveal any part of what you shall hear or see at this time, whether by word, nor put it in writing at any time, nor draw it with the point of a sword, or any other instrument, upon the snow or sand, nor shall you speak of it but with an entered Mason, so help you God.

The most important secret revealed to the initiate during the swearing-in ceremony was the word or sign that enabled him to identify another member of the order, even at a distance, without giving either of them away to outsiders. It was strictly prohibited for a Mason to reveal this secret to anyone who had not joined the society.

Next, the newcomer was counseled by a recent initiate about the tenets of Freemasonry and then, in the words of one account, was "sufficiently frighted with 1000 ridiculous postures and grimaces." Finally, the presiding Mason—in Hall's case, John Batt— inducted the initiate into the society.

Perhaps because the occasion was performed in secrecy, Prince Hall's admission into the Fraternal Order of the Free and Accepted Masons has remained a largely forgotten moment in colonial history. Yet its importance cannot be denied. For the first time in early America, a man of color had set out to organize his people and thereby uplift his race. ❧

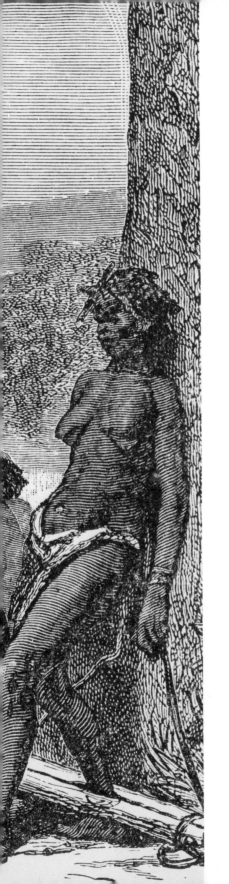

2

"THE IRON YOKE
OF SLAVERY"

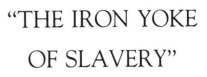

LITTLE IS KNOWN about Prince Hall before he became a slave in 1749 because slave traders did not keep any records of their captives. The only surviving fact about Hall's early years is that he was born in 1735. No one has been able to say exactly where his birthplace was.

Some historians believe Hall was born in the West Indies. A few others claim he was brought to Boston from England. Most likely of all, he was born in West Africa, because that was where the majority of slaves who were transported to North America were caught.

The enslavement of blacks from Africa's west coast—an area that includes the modern nations of Senegal, Guinea, Liberia, Ghana, Nigeria, and Angola—dates back many centuries prior to Hall's time. Indeed, long before the transatlantic slave trade was established, people of all areas, races, and religions had practiced slavery at one time or another. Yet these incidents of slavery were not nearly as

The enslavement of blacks from Africa's west coast became a lucrative business in the 17th century, as European merchants set up a brisk business of exchanging their cargoes of manufactured goods for human beings. Ship captains exchanged their wares for slaves, whom they transported to the West Indies in the Caribbean. Some of the captive Africans remained on the islands; others, after a period of "seasoning," were transported to the American colonies. Prince Hall was among the millions of blacks who were sold into slavery.

systematic as the slave trade that was established after Europeans discovered the New World.

Not long after Christopher Columbus sailed across the Atlantic Ocean in 1492, Europeans started flocking to the Americas, eager to exploit the region's rich agricultural potential. The most profitable crops—sugar, cotton, rice, and tobacco—were also the most labor-intensive, so the settlers began to call for cheap labor. Ready to answer that call were fleets of profit-hungry traders.

Beginning in the early 16th century, shipowners from the Netherlands, Portugal, England, and France established a trade network with several kingdoms along the West African coast. By the 17th century,

Bound by the neck and tied into a human chain, captured villagers are chosen to be auctioned at a slave market. Slave hunters had physicians inspect the Africans for disease, lameness, or any other condition that would limit their value as slaves. Traders would buy only the finest physical specimens because they would fetch the highest prices and also because only the healthy would survive the punishing voyage to the New World.

the European merchants had set up a brisk business of exchanging their cargoes of manufactured goods for human beings. Kingdoms near Ashanti and Dahomey became prosperous by selling prisoners of tribal wars to the European slavers. The coastal African rulers were also known to organize slave-catching expeditions in which inland communities were raided for potential slaves.

To flush their quarry, the African slave hunters often torched entire villages and snared the residents as they fled. The hunters then bound the helpless villagers by their neck and ankles and tied them together in a human chain known as a coffle. These prisoners were marched to the slave markets on the west coast, a trip that sometimes covered hundreds of miles.

Captives who survived the grueling trek were examined, sorted out, and sold. Their hunters usually received cloth, hardware, liquor, or firearms for their efforts.

At first, the slavers transported their prisoners to settlements on the Caribbean islands as well as Mexico and South America. But by the 17th century, British colonists in North America had begun their own large-scale cultivation of cotton, tobacco, and rice and were calling for their own supply of slave labor. The first slaves to reach these colonies (about 20 black Africans) arrived in 1619 aboard a Dutch ship that docked at Jamestown, Virginia. After this initial shipment, the number of slaves in the colonies increased steadily through both importation and reproduction. By the end of the 18th century, Virginia contained about 200,000 blacks.

As the demand for slaves increased in the American colonies, slave trading developed into a highly lucrative business. Ships loaded with rum and other items sailed from New England to Africa's "Slave Coast"; there, the ship captains exchanged their wares for slaves, whom they carried to the West Indies in the Caribbean. Some of the Africans who were delivered to the West Indies remained on the islands. Others, after a period of "seasoning," were transported to the North American colonies.

In exchange for the slaves they left in the West Indies, the ships took on sugar and molasses. On the last leg of this three-part journey, the traders brought the sugar and molasses to New England, where it was distilled into rum. At that point, another slave-trading voyage began.

If Prince Hall was indeed born near Africa's west coast, he would have experienced such a voyage as a teenager. After the punishing march from the interior, he and the other villagers who had managed to stay alive would have been sold by their black captors to the white traders waiting near the shore. The slaves would have then been locked into a barracoon, or stockade, until the traders were ready to have them medically examined. The dozens of barracoons along the coast featured comfortable upstairs quarters for traders and dank, airless pits below for their captives.

Traders usually employed physicians who inspected the captured Africans for disease, lameness, and other conditions that would limit their value as slaves. The traders would buy only the finest physical specimens, partly because these individuals would bring the best prices in the Americas, and partly because only the strong and healthy had much chance of surviving the voyage across the Atlantic Ocean.

Slavers prepare to sell captured Africans at a slave market on the west coast of Africa. Both blacks and whites participated in the African slave trade.

Slave owners marked their new purchases by branding them with a red-hot iron. After being branded, slaves were herded into canoes that ferried them to the ship for the voyage west. Occasionally, slaves managed to escape before they were put on board. An 18th-century slaver noted that "the negroes . . . often leap'd out of the canoos into the sea, and kept under water till they were drowned, to avoid being taken up and saved by our boats." These slaves preferred suicide to the alternative: the horrible voyage from Africa to the West Indies.

Those men and women who were found to be fit were offered at an auction to the English, French, Portuguese, and Dutch ship captains who were waiting to load their vessels with "black gold." After the slaves had been purchased, their new owners had them branded with a red-hot iron. Then they were herded to the shore, where they waited to board the canoe that would ferry them to the slave ship for the voyage west.

Occasionally, slaves managed to break free from their chains before they were put on board. "The negros are so wilful and loth to leave their own country," noted an 18th-century slaver in his journal, "that they have often leap'd out of the canoos into the sea, and kept under water till they were drowned, to avoid being taken up and saved by our boats." These slaves preferred to commit suicide rather than face the horrors of the Middle Passage, the dreaded voyage from Africa to the West Indies.

To prepare for the Middle Passage, slavers packed their human cargo as tightly as possible into the ship's hold. A French writer who visited a slave ship in the mid-17th century noted that some of the captives made the long crossing "lying on their backs" and that they traveled "with their legs bent under them, resting upon the soles of their feet." Crammed into the dark, reeking hold, the slaves were underfed and almost or entirely naked. They had no sanitary facilities, no room to stand, and hardly enough air to breathe.

Although they wasted little sympathy on these unfortunate human beings, the slavers had no wish to see their potentially profitable cargo die. Each day during the 4- to 10-week voyage, the ship's crew took the blacks out on deck for a brief period of exercise and a dousing with seawater. Nevertheless, large numbers—as many as one-half, some historians believe—perished during the transatlantic voyage, succumbing to smallpox, dysentery, malnutrition, and exposure.

The slavers pitched the dead and dying overboard. So many slaves followed this grim path that sharks were said to follow the ships all the way from Africa to America, feeding on the corpses.

Despite the appalling death rate on the slave ships, nearly 10 million Africans survived to become slaves. It is estimated that during the two and a half centuries that the transatlantic slave trade was in operation, 9 million Africans landed in the Caribbean and Central and South America. Nearly half a million Africans arrived on America's shores. So many came, in fact, that they became a significant proportion of the American population.

Existing documents prove that Prince Hall reached America's shores when he was 14 years old. He may have arrived in New England direct from

Africa, or he may have formed part of a boatload of "seasoned" slaves shipped from the West Indies. Whatever his origins, whatever life he led before the age of 14, he himself left no record of it. Like fellow New Englander and former slave Phillis Wheatley, the distinguished poet, Hall remained silent on the subjects of his capture and his arrival in the New World. It is possible that his experiences were too painful to discuss.

The only time Hall ever spoke publicly about the

Slaves were transported from Africa to the West Indies packed into a ship's small hold. Some of the captives made the journey, said one observer, "lying on their backs . . . with their legs bent under them, resting upon the soles of their feet." Underfed and naked, the prisoners had no sanitary facilities, no standing room, and hardly enough air to breathe.

trials of being a slave was in an address he gave at a Masonic lodge in 1797. He talked about Africans who were "dragg'd from their native country by the iron hand of tyranny and oppression, from their dear friends and connections, with weeping eyes and aching hearts, to a strange land and strange people, whose tender mercies are cruel; and there to bear the iron yoke of slavery and cruelty till death as a friend shall relieve them." He may well have been speaking from firsthand experience.

3

A FAITHFUL SERVANT

THE FIRST BLACK slaves to arrive in Massachusetts were brought there in 1638 aboard the British ship *Desire*. By the end of the 17th century, slave traders had established Boston as their main port in the American colonies. A slave coming to New England in 1749, the year Prince Hall arrived, was typically bought at an auction that was held on a wharf near the ship that had carried him or her to America.

For the most part, there was not a great demand for slave labor in Massachusetts or any of the other northernmost colonies. New England's economy was largely based on shipping and manufacturing, industries that did not rely on slave labor. So the majority of the slaves who arrived in New England still had to make one last journey. They were transported to the southern colonies to work as farmhands. Indeed, by the mid-1750s, slaves made up only 2 percent of Massachusetts's population; in contrast, nearly half of the people in Virginia and more than half the population in South Carolina were enslaved blacks.

Hall became one of the comparatively few slaves to remain in Massachusetts. In 1749, he became the property of William Hall, a Boston craftsman, and after being stripped of his African name, was given his owner's surname.

Africans are unloaded from a slave ship that has brought them to Boston. The slave Prince Hall was only 14 years old when he arrived in the city.

A slave's first name was often derived from the job he or she was asked to perform. Accordingly, slaves bore names such as Tinker, Drummer, and Cook. Sometimes, they were called after the day or season in which they were born or after famous people in history. Other slaves were named for an aspect of their character. Thus, it may have been the regal bearing of the teenage slave that inspired William Hall to name him Prince.

Fortunately for young Prince, William Hall was not a brutal or heartless master. Throughout the colonies, there were many ruthless owners who drove their slaves from dawn until dusk. If these slaves tired or protested their treatment, they received punishment that was swift and severe: A whipping followed by a bath of stinging brine was often the means by which an owner tamed an uncooperative slave. On some large farms and plantations, overseers went so far as to patrol the fields with whips and knives to make sure that their slaves worked as hard as possible. It was also common practice for a slave owner to "break a slave's spirit" by selling his or her family members to other slaveholders.

William Hall was nothing like that. A leather dresser by trade, he owned real estate in the vicinity of what is now Post Office Square and was known throughout the community for his civic and philanthropic deeds. In 1737, he joined the Charitable Irish Society of Boston and subsequently became its first elected president.

William Hall and his wife, Margaret, had two daughters, Susannah and Elizabeth, and they all enjoyed the fruits of wealth and high society. But there was no such society in Boston to make the slaves feel welcome. In fact, they enjoyed virtually no legal rights or privileges. Various local laws forbade them to own property, to buy or sell merchandise, to blow horns or beat drums, to sign

Throughout the American colonies, there were many ruthless owners who drove their slaves from dawn until dusk. If these slaves tired or protested, they received swift and cruel punishment: A whipping and then a bath in stinging brine were not unusual occurrences. On some farms and plantations, a slave's family members would be sold to other slaveholders.

contracts, to bear firearms, to drink alcohol, or to congregate in large numbers without the presence of a white.

Blacks, both enslaved and free, were even forbidden to hold church services unless supervised by whites. New Englanders, unlike many of their fellow colonists, allowed blacks to attend church services but required them to sit in a separate section known as the African Corner.

If slaves were lucky, someone might teach them to read and write; otherwise, they did not receive any formal education. In fact, teaching a slave to read and write was a criminal offense in the South.

Slaves were denied the opportunity to go to school, but free blacks were permitted to attend the same classes as whites. One such free black who made the most out of his situation was Benjamin Banneker,

Slaves were denied the opportunity to obtain an education; free blacks, however, were allowed to attend integrated schools in certain areas. Benjamin Banneker, a free black born in Maryland in 1731, attended an integrated school in Baltimore, where he honed his passion for mathematics and science and became a well-known astronomer and surveyor.

who was born four years earlier than Prince Hall, in the British colony of Maryland. Banneker attended an integrated school in the Baltimore area, where he developed a passion for mathematics and astronomy.

Banneker spent most of his days as a tobacco planter; yet he continued to study at night and eventually became widely respected for the scope of his scientific knowledge. In his later years, he compiled a calendar of the different phases of the moon, a chart of the daily position of celestial bodies, and a listing of the times of sunrise, noon, and sunset; then he published these findings in an almanac, a type of book that was indispensable to many early Americans. Banneker's intellectual ability also enabled him to play a significant role in the survey of the land that became the District of Columbia.

Although free blacks were certainly better off than slaves, they remained society's outcasts because their very existence threatened the white majority. Whites maintained that free blacks made slaves more aware of their own limited status and thus contributed to slave insurrections. Around the time of Prince Hall's boyhood, there were several large slave revolts in the colonies. In September 1739, one took place in Stono, South Carolina, where 25 whites were killed before the insurrection was suppressed. The following year, plans for another uprising involving 200 slaves were uncovered in Stono; 50 of them were executed. In March 1741, an incident in New York City led to the deaths of 31 slaves and 5 whites.

Most slaves did not revolt, however, because they were too frightened by the possible consequences if they were caught. So, they worked the long, hard hours demanded by their masters. Prince Hall was fortunate in that he did not have to perform the backbreaking labor many of the field slaves had to endure in the South. Instead, he took on a variety of tasks as a household servant.

Although free blacks were better off than slaves, they remained outcasts in society because whites viewed them as potential leaders of slave revolts. This fear became even more pronounced after a 1741 slave insurrection in New York City led to the death of 31 slaves and 5 whites. Fourteen blacks were burned at the stake as punishment for their participation in the revolt.

Usually, northern slaves became skilled at the trades practiced by their masters. Thus, blacks learned to become carpenters, bricklayers, painters, shoemakers, seamstresses, and blacksmiths. Prince Hall became a leather dresser because that was his master's trade.

A leather dresser's job was to keep leather goods, such as harnesses, supple and free of moisture; otherwise, the leather would dry out and harden. The dressing (the materials applied to the leather) often consisted of chemical solutions that included mineral salts and acids. A leather dresser had to know exactly how much dressing to apply to the skin of an ox, cow, calf, or sheep in order to preserve and protect it.

There was a great need for leather dressing in mid-18th-century Boston. Boasting a variety of industries, it was an extremely lively city. The streets were crowded with men in waistcoats, knee breeches, and white-powdered wigs and with women who wore long, full skirts. The city itself consisted of brick and wood buildings from one to three stories high. By colonial standards, Boston was a sprawling metropolis, even though fewer than 15,000 people lived there.

Like most New Englanders, Bostonians allowed their slave population more liberties than southerners did. Slaves in Massachusetts, for example, were allowed to marry. Hall married for the first time at age 21, when he wedded Delia, a servant who belonged to a neighboring family. The couple had one child, a boy named Primus—Latin for *first*—who became another slave owner's property when he was just one month old. (Like his father, Primus was eventually manumitted, and after serving with distinction in the American Revolution, he joined the same lodge to which Prince Hall belonged.)

Family life, Hall said, made men "happy in having our wives and children like olive branches about our tables." Yet his marrriage to Delia did not last long; she died at an early age.

In November 1763, Hall married another woman, Sarah Ritchie, a servant of Frances Ritchie's. Around that same time, Hall became a member of the Reverend Andrew Croswell's Congregational Church on School Street in Boston. Thus, at the age of 28, he had attained as full a life as any slave could hope for in colonial America: He had a family, knew a trade, and was free to practice his religion.

The city around Prince Hall, though, was full of turmoil. In 1763, there was an outbreak of smallpox in Boston; the disease killed hundreds of people.

Meanwhile, some of the city's working-class whites began to attack the small black population in their midst. "Negro crimes are many," complained one Boston newspaper, "and yet we still keep bringing in those creatures from Guinea; scarce one in a hundred of them good for anything."

Hall witnessed more than his share of beatings and recalled in his later years how "without provocation—twenty or thirty cowards fall upon one man . . . they dare not face you man for man, but in

Slaves working as field hands on plantations in the southern colonies worked long hours and performed backbreaking labor. Hall was fortunate to avoid this fate. Instead, he took on a variety of tasks as a household servant and was taught to be a leather dresser.

a mob." He noted that "these disgraceful and abusive actions [were] committed, not by the men born and bred in Boston, for they are better bred; but by a mob or horde of shameless, low-lived, envious, spiteful persons, some of them not long since, servants in gentlemen's kitchens, scouring knives, tending horses, and driving chaise."

The advice Hall gave to the black community was, "Patience I say, for were we not possess'd of a great measure of it you could not bear up under the

Negroes for Sale

A Cargo of very fine stout Men and Women, in good order and fit for immediate service, just imported from the Windward Coast of Africa, in the Ship Two Brothers.—

Conditions are one half Cash or Produce, the other half payable the first of January next, giving Bond and Security if required.

The Sale to be opened at 10 o'Clock each Day, in Mr. Bourdeaux's *Yard*, at No, 48, on the Bay.

May 19, 1784.   JOHN MITCHELL.

Thirty Seasoned Negroes

To be Sold for Credit, at Private Sale.

AMONGST which is a Carpenter, none of whom are known to be dishonest.

Also; to be sold for Cash, a regular bred young Negroe Man-Cook, born in this Country, who served several Years under an exceeding good French Cook abroad, and his Wife a middle aged Washer-Woman, (both very honest) and their two Children. *Likewise.* a young Man a Carpenter.

For Terms apply to the Printer.

An advertisement for the sale of slaves announces, "A Cargo of very fine stout Men and Women, in good order and fit for immediate service," and emphasizes their skills. Some slaves were taught a trade—including Prince Hall, who learned the art of leather dressing from his master, William Hall.

daily insults you meet with in the streets of Boston;
much more on public days of recreation, how you are
shamefully abus'd, and that at such a degree that you
may truly be said to carry your lives in your hands,
and the arrows of death are flying about your heads."

The greatest cause of unrest in Boston, however,
was the growing conflict between the American
colonists and the occupying troops. The colonies
imported most of their manufactured goods from
England and were forced by the imperial government
to pay high tariffs on them. The situation grew worse
than ever in 1765, when the British Parliament
passed the Stamp Act, a law that required the
colonists to purchase stamps and put them on every
item they printed, including newspapers, pamphlets,
legal documents, and decks of cards.

Taxation without representation became the central complaint of the colonists. In August 1765, a
group of men who called themselves the Sons of
Liberty held a protest through the streets of Boston.
"Liberty! Property, and no stamps!" they shouted as
they made their way to the newly built Stamp Office
building, which they proceeded to tear down. Next,
they ransacked the house of a government official,
stamp collector Andrew Oliver.

Great Britain subsequently repealed the Stamp
Act, but the overall situation failed to improve very
much for the colonists. In 1767, Britain's chief
financial officer, Charles ("Champagne Charlie")
Townsend, imposed a number of severe measures
that bound the business of the colonies even more
tightly to England. The colonists once again complained loudly about these new and drastic measures.
This time, however, British forces were sent to
Boston to keep the public in line.

In most cases, blacks in the American colonies
supported the patriots' cause. Their own circumstances might improve, it was argued, if the colonies

A Faithful Servant   41

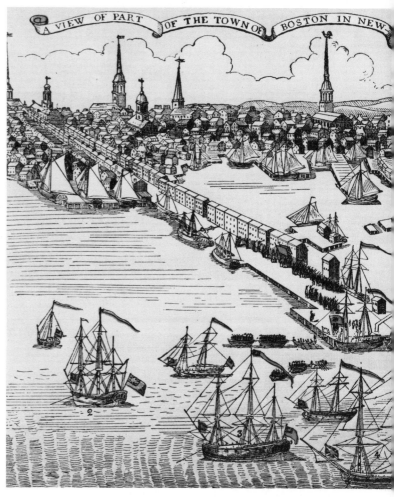

ever gained their independence from England. It was a reasonable hope. Just as the colonists objected to being treated as England's inferiors, so they might come to sympathize with the slaves' plight.

One of the blacks who sided with the colonists was Crispus Attucks, a former slave who had been working as a seaman since he had run away from his Massachusetts master 20 years earlier. On March 5, 1770, Attucks became involved in an incident between a small group of men and boys and a British sentry that became known as the Boston Massacre.

A facsimile of Paul Revere's 1768 engraving of Boston. Depicted in the middle are British warships landing in the harbor.

The colonists began the chain of events by throwing snowballs at a soldier in front of the customs house on King Street. Their attack prompted the main guard, about 20 men, to rush to the redcoat's aid. The citizens of Boston gathered in even larger numbers. Before long, hundreds of them were standing in front of the customs house, taunting the British soldiers. Some of the colonists switched from hurling snowballs to throwing stones.

When one of the sentries was hit by a club, he lowered his musket from his shoulder and, acting without orders, opened fire on the crowd. Following his lead, a few more redcoats let loose several shots. Three colonists immediately fell dead; two others were mortally wounded. Crispus Attucks, one of the most aggressive members of the crowd, was the first to fall. He thus became the first man to die in the American Revolution.

All of Boston was outraged by the soldiers' brutal attack on its citizens. William Hall was no exception. Caught up in the outcry for liberty and equality, he decided to free his slave, Prince Hall.

Just one month after the Boston Massacre, William Hall signed the manumission papers. "Prince Hall has lived with us 21 years," his master wrote, "and served us well upon all occasions for which Reasons we maturely give him his freedom and he is

The greatest cause of unrest in Boston during the 1770s was not race but the growing conflict between the colonists and the occupying British troops. The Boston Massacre, which occurred when British sentries opened fire on a Boston mob on March 5, 1770, strengthened the growing anti-British feeling among the colonists.

Crispus Attucks was one of five civilians shot by British soldiers during the Boston Massacre of 1770. A former slave who had escaped from his Massachusetts master 20 years earlier, he was the first black to die in the American struggle for independence.

no longer to be Reckoned a slave, but has been always accounted as a freeman by us as he has Served us faithfully upon that account we have given him his freedom as witness our hands this Ninth day of April 1770."

At the age of 35, Prince Hall was finally able to take the first steps on the road to freedom. He would soon seek out others to join him on his journey.

4

"THE DYE IS NOW CAST"

Even though Prince Hall was now a free man, he remained as conscious as ever of the evils of slavery. The newspapers were filled with advertisements offering slaves for sale: "To be sold, a tall, likely, straight-limbed negro of twenty-four," read one such announcement. Another said, "Two negro girls of sixteen for sale cheap." Each day, Hall saw slaves sold in public markets. At night, he heard them rattling their leg irons as they passed beneath his window.

Slaves seemed to be everywhere; but so was a growing population of free blacks. Being released from slavery hardly translated into racial equality, however. Many whites regarded blacks who were free the same way they viewed slaves: as lesser beings. As a result, free blacks often had to carry passes indicating that they were not slaves, were widely excluded from the social circles of whites, and were often shunned in the business world.

Nevertheless, a few free blacks in the 18th century achieved significant financial success. Emanuel and Mary Bernoon opened the first oyster and ale house in Providence, Rhode Island, and it quickly became one of the city's most successful establishments. Another black entrepreneur, Samuel Fraunces, founded a tavern in New York City; when George Washington bade farewell to his troops at the end of the American Revolution, he did so at Fraunces Tavern, which is still in operation today.

This early American political cartoon shows 10 Bostonians in a cage hanging from the Liberty Tree, receiving fish and promises from 3 British seamen just before the start of the American Revolution. Cages such as this one were used for punishing slaves as well.

Being freed from slavery did not automatically confer equality to blacks. Many whites regarded free blacks the same way they viewed slaves. Free blacks were excluded from both white social circles and the business world. Southern slave owners required free blacks to wear badges such as these to indicate they were not slaves.

Most free blacks, however, did not enjoy a comfortable existence. They lived in squalid housing and accepted whatever work they could find, no matter how menial it was. Few had the backing needed to start a business. Prince Hall seems to have been one of those lucky few; William Hall apparently helped his former slave begin his own business as a leather dresser.

As Prince Hall settled into his new life, he did so without his second wife, Sarah; she had died of an illness 13 months earlier. Yet he was not alone for very long. On August 22, 1770, just four months after being released from slavery, Hall journeyed to Gloucester, Massachusetts, where the Reverend Samuel Chandler married him to Flora Gibbs. That November, Hall's second son, Prince Africanus, was born.

Meanwhile, the winds of rebellion continued to stir throughout the 13 American colonies. In May 1773, England's Parliament relieved the British East India Company, which Queen Elizabeth I had chartered in 1600 for trade in the Eastern Hemisphere, of paying tariffs on the tea it sold to the colonies. The colonists resented this preferential treatment, which enabled the charter company to monopolize tea sales, and lobbied England to revoke the act. When their protests were ignored, the colonists decided to take the matter into their own hands.

In December 1773, two British East India Company ships carrying a huge cargo of tea sailed into Boston Harbor. Samuel Adams and other patriots immediately asked Governor Thomas Hutchinson to order the ships to return the tea to England. The governor flatly refused their request.

In response, a mob of Bostonians disguised themselves as Mohawks and blacks. Under the cover of night, they descended on the 2 vessels, broke into the cargo holds, and dumped 342 chests of tea into the harbor. This protest became known as the Boston Tea Party.

The destruction of the tea ultimately united the colonists in their call for independence. A deeply angered British Parliament established a series of laws to prevent further incidents of rebellion, including the Boston Port Act, which led to the blockade of Boston Harbor until the destroyed tea had been paid for; the Massachusetts Government Act and the Impartial Administration of Justice Act, both of which put severe limits on the local government's authority; and the Quartering Act, which authorized British officials to commandeer any building to house royal troops. "The dye is now cast," said King George III. "The Colonies must either submit or triumph."

The patriots refused to give in to what they called the Intolerable Acts. In fact, the severe restrictions placed upon them by England prompted all 13 American colonies to band together against the Crown. On September 5, 1774, representatives from each colony convened in Philadelphia to discuss what to do next to combat British rule. These 55 people, who formed the First Continental Congress, issued a Declaration of Rights, which called for the same liberties that the English enjoyed and urged the American colonies to arm themselves against the British.

By the start of 1775, it was clear that fighting would soon break out between the patriots and the British. But once it ended, what situation would blacks find themselves in? Would slavery still exist? Or would blacks in America finally be treated on a par with whites? These were a few of the questions that Prince Hall must have asked himself.

Hall's own hope was that members of his race would be granted a worthy place in American society.

Furthermore, he understood that it was up to him and other blacks to elevate their own status. To bring about any changes, though, they first had to organize themselves, and in 1775 no black organizations existed in any of the colonies.

Even though blacks had been living in the colonies for more than 100 years, whites had not permitted them to set up their own institutions. There were no black churches, schools, newspapers, civic groups, or any other organization of the kind that carried weight with white society. Accordingly, blacks found it almost impossible to join together and draw up effective plans for improving their position.

The only solution was to gain access to an already-established group that might be interested in helping blacks achieve equal rights. Hall believed that Freemasonry, with its emphasis on good fellowship and charitable work, might be that institution. The Masons, he knew, had a long-standing tradition of fighting for noble ideals.

Precisely how long this tradition has existed remains a mystery. According to some historians, Freemasonry began in ancient Egypt. Others claim the institution was born in A.D. 70, when members of a small military unit, the Order of Saint John, bravely defended Jerusalem from invading hordes. These soldiers are said to be the forefathers of the nine young men who traveled to Jerusalem during the First Crusade in 1118 and vowed poverty, chastity, and obedience in their effort to protect the Christian pilgrims who came to the Holy Land. In any event, the ideals of Freemasonry did not become widespread for several centuries.

During the Middle Ages, a freemason was a craftsman who belonged to a guild or company that helped him ply his trade wherever work was available. There were three categories of masons: cowans, or unskilled workers; apprentices; and masters. It took

This chart displays the three categories of Freemasonry: cowans, or unskilled workers; apprentices; and masters. It took an apprentice several years to earn the privilege of calling himself a master.

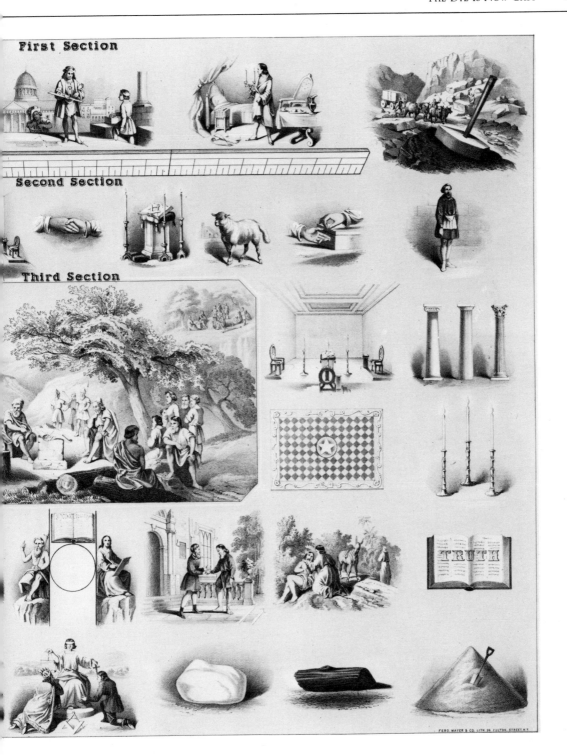

First Section

Second Section

Third Section

an apprentice several years to earn the right to call himself a master.

A good part of a mason's day centered around the lodge, a workshop that also served as a place where he could relax, drink, and converse with other craftsmen. The secret signal that Masons have used for centuries to hail one another probably came into existence as a way for a skilled mason to determine at a moment's notice if another person had received similar training. All a medieval mason had to do was use the masonic handgrip, utter the masonic word or phrase, or display a masonic emblem. If the other man gave the appropriate response, then he, too, was a skilled mason.

Among the Masonic emblems is the staring eye, which signifies the deity whom Masons call the Great Architect of the Universe. This deity, explained one Mason, "governs all things here below by his almighty power, and his watchful eye is over all our works." The Masonic eye even watches over daily business transactions; it appears on the back of every one-dollar bill.

Other Masonic symbols are two compasses, reminders that desires and passions must be contained; an orb of light, which designates truth; and two beavers, which represent industry. There is also a Masonic motto: Follow Reason.

The founding of the first grand lodge, the governing body of modern-day Freemasonry, took place on June 24, 1717, when four lodges in London joined together. Within a dozen years, other grand lodges were established in India, Ireland, and the West Indies. The first lodges to be formed in America were set up in Philadelphia (1730) and Boston (1733).

As Freemasonry expanded across the globe in the 18th century, its membership also increased. A historian of the time, the Reverend James Anderson, noted in *The Constitutions of the Free-Masons* (1723) that in his day Masons were not compelled to believe in the Holy Trinity of the Christian faith, as they were decades earlier. Instead, Freemasonry had been opened up to men "by whatever Denominations or Persuasions they may be distinguish'd."

Freemasonry's emphasis on religious tolerance was one of the reasons the institution gained acceptance in the American colonies. It appealed to people who were in search of spiritual guidance as well as those who felt estranged from Mother England. Moreover, it allowed the socially ambitious to join an exclusive society. Among the most notable early Americans who became Masons were Benjamin Franklin, who was elected grand master of the Pennsylvania Masons in 1734, and George Washington.

In this depiction of Masonic emblems, the staring eye (at top) signifies the deity whom the Masons call the Great Architect of the Universe. This deity is said to govern all earthly actions, even business transactions. Accordingly, the Masonic eye appears on the back of every one-dollar bill.

Freemasonry appealed to people in search of spiritual guidance as well as to those who felt estranged from Mother England. Moreover, it allowed the socially ambitious to join an exclusive society. Among the most notable early Americans who became Masons were Benjamin Franklin, who was elected grand master of the Pennnsylvania Masons in 1734, and George Washington, the first president of the United States.

Like most nonmembers, Hall greatly admired the people who were said to be members of the order. To become a Mason, a person had to be clear thinking and had to have a social conscience. Such people, Hall was certain, could do more than any other group to help blacks in their struggle for racial equality.

It is not known exactly how or when Hall learned of Freemasonry. His master, William Hall, may have been a Mason or may have been acquainted with some members of the order, or else Prince Hall may have had some friends who were Masons. In any case, it occurred to Hall that he might be able to help the black cause if he could join the order and win the fellowship of its vast international membership. It did not escape his notice, however, that although the institution supported the idea of brotherhood, it did not accept any blacks as members.

In spite of the Masons' refusal to admit blacks, Hall believed that they would accept him into their order. If a war was going to take place between the colonies and a great world power, the American patriots would want to make use of every available person to fight against England. One way to get blacks to join the side of the colonists was to show them they had a vested interest in fighting for independence. The colonists might do this, Hall felt, by integrating some of their institutions.

In 1775, when Hall decided to apply for membership as a Mason, there were about 150 Masonic lodges in the American colonies. Many of these lodges doubled as military outposts and communication centers for the rebels, relaying vital information from lodge to lodge. Yet none of these lodges was willing to admit Hall when he requested to join the order. Every lodge he approached turned him down.

Eventually, Hall decided on another course of action. He went to British Army Lodge No. 441, where he knew some Masons were stationed, and arranged to be inducted into the order along with 14 other blacks. On March 17, 1775—11 days after he was officially made a Mason—Hall received a permit from fellow Mason John Batt to establish a separate lodge for blacks. Hall formed his own unit, the African Lodge, on July 3. This lodge would eventually become the foundation of black Freemasonry in America. ❧

5

"GIVE THEM
THEIR FREEDOM"

IN THE SUMMER of 1775, Prince Hall began to seek out the most highly regarded members of Boston's free black society to join the newly formed African Lodge. But it was not an easy task. He lacked a sizable pool of applicants from which to choose because the local free black population was not very large. In addition, there was not a black upper class to recruit from; the social structure of colonial America did not allow blacks to attain positions of high standing in the community. All Hall could do was apply his own strict standards of judgment and solicit those men who struck him as hardworking and freethinking.

The start of the American Revolution also made it difficult for Hall to build up the lodge. British troops and the patriot militia had clashed for the first time on April 19, 1775, at Lexington, Massachusetts. This skirmish was followed by several more confrontations in the Boston area, including the Battle of Bunker Hill. During that encounter, Major General

British troops and the patriot militia clashed for the first time on April 19, 1775, at Lexington, Massachusetts. Eight Americans were killed in the battle; however, by the end of the day, the British had lost three times as many men as the Americans.

Thomas Gage and his redcoats drove the colonists from their position overlooking Boston Harbor, but not before the British suffered their heaviest losses of the war. The British won the battle but had 1,054 casualties to the Americans' 441.

Hall most likely did not take part in any of these campaigns because blacks were banned from enlisting in the militia. At the Second Contintental Congress, 43-year-old George Washington, commander of the patriots' forces, the Continental army, put into effect the General Militia Act. This law declared that "neither Negroes, boys unable to bear arms, nor old men unfit to endure the fatigue of the campaign are to be enlisted."

Washington, a prosperous Virginia planter who owned more than 200 slaves, did not doubt that blacks were fit to bear arms. (Indeed, despite the

British troops clashed with colonial minutemen on April 19, 1775, on North Bridge, in Concord, a few miles outside Boston. This battle occurred when Governor Thomas Gage learned that the Massachusetts colonists had stockpiled a large supply of munitions at Concord. Gage dispatched about 1,000 British troops to Concord, where they destroyed the colonists' arsenal.

prohibition, some of them already had.) His concern was just the opposite: He feared that armed slaves might begin a rebellion of their own. In addition, Washington believed that keeping the slaves at work in the fields was essential for maintaining a strong economy during wartime.

According to some accounts, Prince Hall tried to persuade Washington to allow blacks into the army. It has been said that Hall headed a contingent of free blacks who met with the general after he took command of the Continental army on July 3, 1775. If such a meeting did in fact take place, Hall did not achieve the outcome he desired.

One notable black from Boston who did meet with Washington in the early stages of the revolution was Phillis Wheatley, America's first black poet. Slave traders had kidnapped her from Africa in 1761, when she was seven years old, and had sold her to the wealthy Wheatley family of Boston. There she mastered the English language and began to write verse. By the time Wheatley was a teenager, she was a well-known writer who recited her poems for the New England elite. Her only book, *Poems on Various Subjects, Religious and Moral*, was published in 1773 and brought her widespread acclaim.

On a brisk March day in 1776, Wheatley visited with Washington at his headquarters in Cambridge, a Massachusetts town near Boston. The general had invited Wheatley to Cambridge after reading a 42-line poem she had written about him. Wheatley's poem ended with a ringing tribute to the newly appointed commander:

Proceed, great chief, with virtue on thy side,
Thy ev'ry action let the Goddess guide.
A crown, a mansion, and a throne that shine,
With gold unfading, WASHINGTON! be thine.

No record exists of the 30-minute conference that Wheatley had with Washington. Yet Wheatley, who had been a slave until she was 21 years old, was an outspoken opponent of slavery. In fact, in 1774 she became one of the first blacks in America to publish a scathing attack on slavery. But not even Wheatley, one of colonial America's most highly esteemed blacks, could persuade Washington to alter his views on slavery, especially when most revolutionary leaders agreed with him that blacks should not be allowed to join the Contintental army.

George Washington inspects the work of slaves at Mount Vernon, his Virginia plantation. Washington had banned blacks from enlisting in the militia for fear that armed slaves would incite rebellions. Washington owned more than 200 slaves and believed that keeping slaves at work in the fields was essential to a strong wartime economy.

One of the few American leaders who thought blacks should play an active role in the struggle for independence from England was John Hancock, president of the Continental Congress. If the colonists did not "give them their freedom with their sword," he observed, "the enemy probably will."

Hancock was right. On November 7, 1775, British commanders formally invited slaves and free blacks to join their side. A show of loyalty to the Crown, the British authorities said, would be rewarded with freedom.

President of the Continental Congress, John Hancock was one of the few American leaders who believed blacks should be permitted to enlist in the colonial militia. Hancock believed that if the colonists did not "give them their freedom with their sword, the enemy probably will." He was proved correct: On November 7, 1775, British commanders formally invited slaves and free blacks to join their side.

This offer of manumission appealed especially to blacks in the South. For example, thousands of slaves in South Carolina and Georgia left their plantations between 1775 and 1783 to join the British army. Some of them became soldiers, guides, and spies. Most of these runaways, however, found themselves stuck in menial jobs, having to handle the same chores they had performed as slaves.

Although these former slaves did not see their fortunes improve along with allegiance to the British army, their mass defections clearly detracted from the patriots' war effort. One by one, American leaders acknowledged the need to increase the size of their own army if they wanted to defeat the large and powerful British forces. The British were in the process of sending 60,000 soldiers across the Atlantic Ocean to fight the patriots.

Beginning in 1776, several American colonies began to permit blacks to fight alongside whites. Two years later, Massachusetts joined the group of colonies that legally incorporated blacks into the militia. In fact, by 1778, blacks in Massachusetts were not only permitted to fight but were commanded to do so. Military service was required of "any person living or residing in any town or plantation within this state the term of three months together."

Hall joined the Massachusetts militia in 1776, two years before it was mandatory for blacks in Massachusetts to join the Continental army. "At the breaking-out of the war," Captain George W. Williams said of

Phillis Wheatley, America's first black poet, was kidnapped from Africa when she was only seven years old and sold to the Wheatley family of Boston. She quickly mastered the English language and in 1773 published her only book, Poems on Various Subjects, Religious and Moral. In 1776, General Washington, captivated by a poem she had written about him, invited Wheatley to meet with him in Cambridge.

As Washington prepares to review his troops, a young black soldier holds the reins of his horse. Washington finally authorized the enlistment of blacks in 1776.

Hall, "he was residing at Dartmouth. His first enlistment was in January or February, 1776, in Capt. Benjamin Dillingham's company." Between his stints in the army, Hall continued his work as a leather dresser.

When Hall joined the Contintental army, at age 41, he became one of the more than 5,000 blacks who wound up serving under George Washington's command. Most of them were assigned the rank of private, a position without much responsibility. Like the blacks who joined up with the British, they were forced to undertake menial but essential work, such as digging trenches and tending horses. Very few blacks were assigned to the cavalry, the army's most glamorous branch. Indeed, some of the soldiers who had been slaves were not even granted the honor of seeing their own name listed on the army's rolls. Instead, they were recorded as "a Negro man" or "a Negro, name not known."

Even though few blacks were granted the opportunity to fight in the field, several blacks who fought in the American Revolution managed to win praise for their heroic acts. Among them were William Flora, who was the very last sentinel to retreat from the British at the Battle of Great Bridge in Virginia, and Jack Sisson, who was among a group of volunteers that captured a British general at his headquarters near Newport, Rhode Island, in July 1777.

According to Captain Williams, Hall "must have been a man of more than ordinary talents." Little is known, however, about his war record. The only existing account of Hall's experiences as a soldier comes from an address he gave to his fellow Masons in 1792: "Whether there may be any so weak, or rather so foolish, as to say, because they were blacks that would make their lodge or army too common or too cheap?" Hall asked. "Sure this was not our conduct in the late war; for then they marched shoulder to shoulder, brother soldier and brother soldier to the field of battle; let who will answer; he that despises a black man for the sake of his colour, reproaches his maker."

It was precisely these kinds of sentiments that prompted Hall to link forces with seven other men— three of whom were Masons—on January 13, 1777, and sign a petition that called for "an act of the legislature whereby [blacks] may be restored to the

A list of the names of those who were killed and wounded at the Battle of Concord. Most blacks who joined the Continental army were assigned the lowly rank of private and given menial tasks, such as digging trenches. Some of the soldiers who had been slaves were not even granted the honor of seeing their own name listed on the army's roll. Instead, they were recorded as "a Negro man" or "a Negro, name not known."

The Bucks of America, an all-black Massachusetts company, carried this flag into battle during the American Revolution. Of the 300,000 men who fought for American independence, about 5,000 were black.

enjoyment of that freedom which is the natural right of all men and that their children, who were born in this land—may not be held as slaves after they arrive at twenty one years." Claiming that slavery was not consistent with the patriots' ideals of liberty and independence, they sent the petition to the Massachusetts legislature, which in turn forwarded the document to the Continental Congress. There it received a cold reception. Massachusetts did not outlaw the slave trade until 1788, the same year that it became the sixth state to join the Union. Slavery itself was not abolished in the state until a few years later, nearly a decade after the end of the American Revolution.

The fighting, for the most part, concluded on October 19, 1781, when 8,000 British troops surrendered their arms to General Washington after being heavily bombarded by artillery at Yorktown, Virginia. Reluctant to continue a prolonged war on foreign soil against a large and well-equipped army, the British agreed in 1782 to hold preliminary peace negotiations with American representatives John Adams, Benjamin Franklin, John Jay, and others in Paris.

The final terms of the Treaty of Paris were hammered out the following year, and the treaty was signed on September 3, 1783. The treaty acknowledged the independence of the American colonies and granted the new nation the entire region between the Atlantic Ocean and the Mississippi River. The Continental Congress ratified the accord on January 14, 1784.

Throuogut the land, Americans could now point with pride to their stirring triumph. Yet for Prince Hall and other blacks, the struggle for freedom was far from over. ✺

6

WAITING FOR THE CHARTER

T HE MASONIC LODGES in the United States declared their independence from the English Grand Lodge and formed their own organizational structure in 1781. Prince Hall subsequently approached a few of the local lodges, much as he had done nearly a decade earlier. This time, however, he was not seeking to become a Mason. He wanted to connect his lodge to the American Grand Lodge. And for that to happen, he needed the authority of an established Masonic order to grant him a charter.

While Hall searched for a lodge that would admit black Masons into the fraternity of American Free-masonry, he met regularly with the members of the African Lodge. These meetings were held at Hall's tannery shop, the Golden Fleece, on Water Street. On December 31, 1782, a Boston newspaper published the following account of one of the lodge's activities.

British general Charles Cornwallis, the commander of 8,000 British troops, surrenders to General George Washington after the colonists' decisive victory at Yorktown, Virginia, on October 19, 1781. A few minor battles remained to be fought, but after this surrender, the American Revolution was effectively over.

On Friday last, 27th, the Feast of St. John the Evangelist, was celebrated by St. Black's Lodge of Free and Accepted Masons, who went in procession preceded by a band of music, dressed in their [Masonic] aprons and jewels from Brother G[al]pion up State Street and thru Cornhill to the House of the Right Worshipful Grand Master in Water Street, where an elegant and splendid entertainment was given upon the occasion.

Apparently, this account of the ceremony displeased Hall. To set the record straight, he wrote a letter to the publisher of the newspaper.

> Sir: Observing a sketch in Monday's paper printed by Mess Draper and Folsom, relative to the celebration of the feast of St. John the Evangelist by the African Lodge, the Master of said Lodge being possessed of a charitable disposition of all mankind, does therefore hope the publisher of the said sketch meant to give a candid description of the procession, etc. Therefore with due submission to the public, our title is not St. Black's Lodge, neither do we aspire after high titles. But our only desire is that the Great Architect of the universe would diffuse in our hearts the true spirit of masonry, which is love of God and universal love to all mankind. These I humbly conceive to be the two grand pillars of Masonry. Instead of a splendid entertainment, we had an agreeable one on brotherly love.
>
> With humble submission to the above publishers and the public I beg leave to subscribe myself
>
> Your humble servant,
> Prince Hall
> Master of African Lodge

Unfortunately for Hall, his attempts to promote brotherly love meant little to the lodges he approached for a charter. Every lodge refused his request to sanction the African Lodge. Indeed, Hall may have wondered if he would have been better off joining the many blacks who left the colonies for England in 1782 and 1783. His dream that the American Revolution might prompt whites to grant blacks equal rights had not come true. White Masons still insisted on excluding blacks from their ranks.

Left with no alternative but to seek outside help in getting his lodge sanctioned, Hall turned to a Masonic order that was based abroad. He was by no means the first person in America to try this approach. Nearly 30 years earlier, in 1756, 7 Masons in the American colonies who had been denied a charter decided to seek authorization from a Masonic lodge overseas. It took three years for the Grand Lodge of Scotland to investigate whether or not these men should be allowed to establish their own lodge. Finally, in 1759, they were granted a charter.

Well aware of this episode, Hall sat down in early March 1784 and made out an application for a charter to a man with whom he may have already been acquainted, William Moody, the Most Worshipful Master of Brotherly Love at Lodge No. 55 in London, England. Hall wrote to Moody:

Most Worshipful Sir: Permit me to Return to you my Brotherly Love and Gratitude for your kindness to my Brethren when in a strange land. When in time of need you stood their friend and Brother (as they inform me), and as much as you have done it to them I take it as done to me, for which I now Beg leave to return you, the Wardens and Rest of the Brethren of your lodge my hearty thanks. I hope you will forgive whatsoever you may have seen amiss in them.

Dear Brother we hope that you will not receive no Brother of our Lodge without his warrant, and signed in manner and form as B'Reed.

Dear Brother I would inform you that this Lodge hath been founded almost eight years and we have had only a Permit to Walk on St. John's Day and to Bury our Dead in manner and form. We have had no opportunity to apply for a Warrant before now, though we have been importuned to send to France for one, yet we thought it best to send to the Fountain from whence we received the Light for a Warrant; and now Dear Br. we must make you our advocate at the Grand Lodge, hoping you will be so good (in our name and Stead) to Lay this Before the Royal Grand Master and the Grand Wardens and the rest of the Grand Lodge; who we hope will not deny us nor treat us Beneath the rest of our fellowmen, although Poor yet Sincere Brethren of the Craft. After wishing you all happiness here and hereafter, I beg leave to subscribe myself your Loving Friend and Brother.

Prince Hall
Boston, March 2, 1784.

On September 29, 1784, William Moody issued a charter for Hall's lodge. "Know ye," read part of the charter, "that we, at the humble petition of our Right Trusty and well-beloved Brethren, Prince Hall, Boston Smith, Thomas Sanderson and several other

Daniel Shays, a veteran of the American Revolution, launched a 1786 rebellion against Massachusetts because the state had imposed high taxes on many of its farmers. Hall and his Masonic brothers offered to help repel this band of rebels.

Brethren, residing in Boston, New England in North America, do hereby constitute the said Brethren into a regular Lodge of Free and Accepted Masons, under the title or denomination of the African Lodge."

Hall, the charter also said, was appointed Master

of the lodge, whose full name was African Lodge No. 459. As Master of the lodge, he was charged with the following responsibilities:

We hereby will and require you, the said Prince Hall, to take special care that all and every said Brethren are or have been regularly made Masons, and that they do observe, perform and keep all the rules and orders contained in the Book of Constitutions, and further, that you do, from time to time, cause to be entered in a book kept for that purpose, an account of your proceedings in the lodge together with all such rules, orders and regulations, as shall be made for the good government of the same, that in no

James Bowdoin, the governor of Massachusetts, refused Hall's offer of the use of his Masonic brothers to help put down Shays's Rebellion. Hall had written to the governor: "We, though unworthy members of this commonwealth are willing to help and support so far as our weak and feeble abilities may become necessary in this time of trouble and confusion."

wise you omit once in every year to send to us, or our successors, Grand Masters or to . . . our Deputy Grand Master, for the time being an account in writing of your said proceedings.

But Hall was unable to perform these duties right away. It took three years for the charter to travel across the Atlantic Ocean and reach him. On May 2, 1787, immediately after Captain James Scott, a brother-in-law of John Hancock's, delivered the document, Hall wrote to the *Massachusetts Sentinel* that "his Royal Highness, the Duke of Cumberland, and the Grand Lodge have been graciously pleased to grant the African Lodge in Boston as the Brethren." Hall added that "by the Grace of God, I also endeavor to fulfill all that is required of me in the charter and as I shall make the constitution my guide, I hope we shall adorn our profession as Masons."

Hall had already indicated the lodge's willingness "to be peaceable subjects to the Civil power where we reside" a year earlier. In 1786, Daniel Shays, a veteran of the American Revolution, launched a rebellion against the Massachusetts government because it had imposed high taxes on many of its farmers. Hall promptly offered the services of himself and his fellow Masons to Massachusetts governor James Bowdoin in putting down the insurrection. On November 26, 1786, Hall wrote to the governor, "We, though unworthy members of this Commonwealth are willing to help and support so far as our weak and feeble abilities may become necessary in this time of trouble and confusion." Much to Hall's disappointment, Bowdoin rejected his offer and chose to break up Shays's Rebellion without the help of a black militia.

By then, Hall had made yet another effort to better the lives of his fellow blacks. On January 4, 1787, he signed a petition requesting the General

In 1815, Paul Cuffe, shipping magnate and abolitionist, brought a group of black Bostonian homesteaders to the West African colony of Sierra Leone, where he hoped to develop a prosperous mercantile center. This silhouette commemorates one of Cuffe's voyages.

Court of Massachusetts to allow blacks to return to Africa. Part of the petition stated:

> That we, or our ancestors have been taken from all our dear connections and brought from Africa and put into a state of slavery in this country; from which unhappy situation we have been lately in some measure delivered by the new constitution which has been adopted by this state, or by a free act of our former masters. But we yet find ourselves in many respects in very disagreeable disadvantageous circumstances; most of which must attend us so long as we and our children live in America.
>
> This, and other considerations which we need not here particularly mention, induce us earnestly to desire our return to Africa our native country, which warm climate is

much more agreeable to us; and where we shall live among our equals and be more comfortable and happy than we can be in our present situation; and at the same time may have a prospect of usefulness to our brethren there—The soil of our native country is good and produces the necessaries of life in great abundance—when this shall be effected by a number of blacks sent there for this purpose who shall be thought most capable of making such application and transacting this business then they who are disposed to go and settle there shall form themselves into a civil society, united by a political constitution, and shall be thought qualified, shall unite and be formed into a religious society or christian church.

Signed by Hall and 72 others, the petition did not mark the first time in American history that blacks had requested permission to return to Africa. But no previous document had ever asked for aid in establishing a black colony in Africa. The petition contained several suggestions for financing the colony, including a proposal to place a part of a slave's daily wages in a fund that would help pay the cost of his or her voyage to Africa.

The petitioners never received a reply to their request. Yet the dream of establishing a colony in Africa would become a reality shortly after Hall's lifetime. In 1811, Paul Cuffe, a shipping entrepreneur and antislavery crusader, made an exploratory voyage to the West African colony of Sierra Leone, where he hoped black settlers from America could set up a thriving mercantile center. He made another trip to Sierra Leone four years later. This time, Cuffe brought with him a group of black homesteaders from Boston.

CAUTION!!

COLORED PEOPLE

OF BOSTON, ONE & ALL,

You are hereby respectfully CAUTIONED and advised, to avoid conversing with the

Watchmen and Police Officers of Boston,

For since the recent ORDER OF THE MAYOR & ALDERMEN, they are empowered to act as

KIDNAPPERS

AND

Slave Catchers,

And they have already been actually employed in KIDNAPPING, CATCHING, AND KEEPING SLAVES. Therefore, if you value your LIBERTY, and the *Welfare of the Fugitives* among you, *Shun* them in every possible manner, as so many *HOUNDS* on the track of the most unfortunate of your race.

Keep a Sharp Look Out for KIDNAPPERS, and have TOP EYE open.

APRIL 24, 1851.

7

"LIVE AND ACT AS MASONS"

A bill cautioning the free blacks of Boston to beware of watchmen and police officers who were empowered to kidnap and enslave them. In 1778, Hall worked successfully for the release of three free blacks who had been kidnapped by a sea captain and sold into slavery. Hall wrote in a petition to the General Court of Massachusetts: "What then are our lives and liberties worth, if they may be taken away in such a cruel and unjust manner as this?"

BY THE TIME Prince Hall received the charter for the African Lodge in 1787, he was already seeking to help the black community in other ways besides expanding his lodge. One of his main objectives was to help educate young blacks in the Boston area. Although blacks paid the same taxes as whites, they received, as Hall put it, "no benefit from the free schools of Boston." He was determined that "means be provided for the education of colored people."

On October 17, 1787, Hall and other concerned blacks filed a petition with the Massachusetts legislature that drew attention to the fact that while blacks paid their taxes promptly, only whites were offered facilities to educate their children. This petition, written by Hall, pointed out that black children suffered a great disadvantage because they were denied schooling. "We, therefore, must fear for our raising offspring to see them in a land of gospel light," he wrote, "when there is provision made for them as well as others and yet can't enjoy and for no other reason can be given this, they are black." The legislature ignored this appeal.

Hall, however, refused to stop fighting on behalf of the black community. On February 27, 1788, he and 20 other blacks sent another petition to the

General Court of Massachusetts, this time about a matter involving Solomon Babson, captain of the sloop *Ruby*. That winter, the captain had kidnapped three free blacks and sold them into slavery. His actions so outraged Hall and the others that they wrote in their petition:

> The Petition of a number of Blacks, freemen of this commonwealth, humbly showeth:
>
> That your petitioners are justly alarmed at the inhuman and cruel treatment that three of our brethren, free citizens of the town of Boston, lately received. The captain, under pretense that this vessel was in distress on an Island below in this harbour, having got them on board, put them in irons, and carried them off from their wives and children, to be sold as slaves. This being the unhappy state of these poor men, what can your petitioners expect but to be treated in the same manner by the same sort of men? What then are our lives and liberties worth, if they may be taken away in such a cruel and unjust manner as this? May it please your honours, we are not insensible that the good laws of this state, forbid all such bad actions; notwithstanding, we can assure your honours, that many of our free blacks, that have entered on board vessels as seamen have been sold for slaves, and some of them we have heard from; but know not who carried them away! Hence, it is, that many of us, who are good seamen, are obliged to stay at home through fear, and one-half of our time loiter about the streets, for want of employ; whereas, if they were protected in that lawful calling, they might get a handsome livelihood for themselves and theirs, which in the situation they are now in, they cannot.

The petitioners had one other point to make:

> One thing more we would beg leave to hint: that is, that your petitioners have for sometime past, beheld with grief, ships cleared out from this harbour for Africa, and they either steal our brothers and sisters, fill their ship-holds full of unhappy men and women, crowded together, then set out for the best market to sell them there, like sheep for slaughter and then return here like honest men, after having sported with the lives and liberty of their fellow-

men, and at the same time call themselves christians. Blush
O Heavens at this! These, our weighty grievances we
cheerfully submit to your Honours, without dictating in the
least, knowing by experiences that your Honours have, and
we trust ever will, in your wisdom, do us that justice that
our present condition requires as God and the good laws of
this commonwealth shall dictate to you.

When the text of this petition was published a
few months later in the *American Mercury*, only one
signature appeared under it: Prince Hall's. Yet he was
not alone in expressing his outrage. An antislavery
movement led by the Society of Friends—or Quakers,
as they are popularly known—had begun to spread
across the country. Dedicated to religious and social
freedom, the Quakers had become the first Christian
denomination in the United States to forbid its
members to own slaves.

The Quakers responded to Hall's petition by
sending their own petition to the Massachusetts
legislature, "praying that measures might be taken for
preventing the slave trade." Other groups and organizations, including the Boston Association of Ministers, also petitioned to outlaw the slave trade.

Together, these protests drew a positive response.
On March 26, 1788, the Massachusetts legislature
passed an act "to prevent the Slave-Trade and for
granting Relief to the Families of such unhappy
Persons as may be Kidnapped or decoyed away from
this commonwealth." The law stated that "no citizen
of this Commonwealth or other person residing
within the same shall import, transport, buy, or sell
any of the inhabitants of Africa, as slaves or servants." In Massachusetts, at least, free blacks had
succeeded in helping to abolish the slave trade.

Hall was especially pleased. The banning of the
slave trade was proof that blacks were finally on their
way to gaining equal rights. The process might be
slow, but it was not hopeless.

Meanwhile, John Hancock and other officials in Boston worked to obtain the release of the three men who had been captured by Captain Babson and sold into slavery on the island of St. Barthélemy. Dr. Jeremy Belknap, a prominent antislavery activist in Boston, described this turn of events in a letter to Dr. Benjamin Rush:

> I have one good piece of news to tell you. The Negroes who were kidnapped from here last winter have returned. . . . The morning after their arrival here, they made me a visit

The Society of Friends, better known as the Quakers, were early leaders of the antislavery movement that spread across America. Great believers in religious and social freedom, the Quakers became the first Christian denomination in the United States to require the expulsion of slave-owning members.

being introduced by Prince Hall, who is *Primus Interparese* [First Interpreter] of the blacks in this town. The interview was affecting. There, said Prince, is the gentleman that was so much your friend and petitioned the court for us. They joined in thanking me.

Hall helped celebrate the release of the three men by organizing a welcome home party for them. Meanwhile, he looked for larger quarters to serve as the meeting place of the African Lodge because its membership had continued to grow. When the lodge made plans to hold its Saint John's Day celebration in 1789, Hall received permission from Boston officials to rent out Faneuil Hall, a large public building that had served as a headquarters for the patriots during the American Revolution.

Helping Hall preside over the Saint John's Day celebration was the Reverend John Marrant, an Englishman who had served as a missionary to the Cherokee, the Catawar, the Housaw, and other Native American tribes. Marrant had recently agreed to serve as the lodge's chaplain. Hall, he claimed, was "one of the most respected characters in Boston."

One of the ways that Hall won this respect was by continuing to fight for black education. "Let us lay by our recreations and all superfluities," he said, "so that we may have that money to educate our rising generation which was spent in these follies. Make you this beginning, and who knows but God may raise up some friend or body of friends, as he did in Philadelphia, to open a school for blacks here, as that friendly city has done."

Hall's mention of Philadelphia was in reference to the Free African Society, a nonreligious organization founded by the Reverend Absalom Jones and the Reverend Richard Allen to serve their city's black community. Among the Free African Society's achievements was its success in sponsoring several education projects for Philadelphia's black residents. Like Hall, Jones and Allen had become pillars of their community. But whereas Hall operated through the Masonic lodge, the two ministers worked through the church. In 1804, the Boston-born Jones, who was a friend of Hall's, became America's first black Episcopal priest. Twelve years later, Allen formed the African Methodist Episcopal church and was elected its first bishop.

As for the African Lodge, Hall and the other black Masons continued to go about their business

Richard Allen, a Methodist preacher, was a leading citizen of Philadelphia's black community. Together with the Reverend Absalom Jones, they founded the Free African Society, a nonreligious organization dedicated to serving Philadelphia's black population. In 1816, Allen formed the African Methodist Episcopal (AME) church and was elected its first bishop.

without any help from their white brethren. As a white Mason wrote to Belknap, "The African lodge in Boston tho possessing a charter from England, meet by themselves, and white Masons not more skilled in Geometry than their black brethren will not acknowledge them."

Belknap himself, writing an overview of Hall's organization, got to the heart of the matter: "Some white brethren have visited this lodge, but none of the blacks have yet visited the lodges of the white brethren, nor do I know that they ever applied and been refused. . . . The truth is, they are *ashamed* of being on a equality with blacks. . . . Masonry considers all men equal who are free and Massachusetts Laws admit of no kind of slavery. It is evident from this, that neither avowedly nor tacitly do the blacks admit the preeminence of the whites, but it is evident that a preeminence is claimed by the whites."

Hall publicly expressed his feelings about this and other issues on June 25, 1792, in "A Charge Delivered to the Brethren of the African Lodge," which he gave at a lodge in Charlestown, Massachusetts. First, he called attention to

the duty of a Mason; and the first thing is, that he believes in one Supreme Being, that he is the great Architect of this visible world, and that he governs all things here below by his almighty power, and his watchful eye is over all our works. Again we must be good subjects to the laws of the land in which we dwell, giving honour to whom honour is due; and that we have no hand in any plots or conspiracies or rebellion, or side or assist in them: for when we consider the bloodshed, the devastation of towns and cities that hath been done by them, what heart can be so hard as not to pity those our distrest brethren, and keep at the greatest distance from them. However just it may be on the side of

A white schoolmaster bars the admission of black students in this illustration from an early-19th-century abolitionist journal. Although blacks paid the same taxes as whites, they received, Hall said, "no benefit from the free schools of Boston." Only whites were offered facilities to educate their children. This situation was intolerable to Hall, who in 1800 recruited two Harvard University students to act as teachers for a school for blacks that he opened in his own home. Thus, Hall became the founder of Boston's first black school.

the opprest, yet it doth not in the least, or rather ought not, abate that love and fellow-feeling which we ought to have for our brother fellow men.

The next thing is love and benevolence to all the family of mankind, as God's make and creation, therefore we ought to love them all.

Hall pointed out in this address that another feature of Freemasonry was the obligation of every Mason to attend the meetings:

The duty of a Mason is, that he pays a strict regard to the stated meetings of the Lodge, for masonry is of a progressive nature, and must be attended to if ever he intends to be a good Mason; for the man that thinks that because he hath been made a Mason, and is so called, and at the same time will willfully neglect to attend his Lodge, he may be assured he will never make a good Mason, nor ought he to be looked upon as a good member of the craft. . . . Another thing a Mason ought to observe, is that he should lend his helping hand to a brother in distress, and relieve him; this we may do various ways—for we may sometimes help him to a cup of cold water, and it may be better to him than a cup of wine.

In 1796, Hall made another appeal to Boston officials for the establishment of a black school. They approved his request but then said they could not find a building to house the school. As disappointed as Hall was, he could at least take consolation in that he now knew of some officials who claimed to be on his side.

By 1797, seven black schools had been established in Philadelphia, while Boston still possessed none. This situation prompted Hall to come up with a second "Charge Delivered to the Brethren of the African Lodge." He gave this address on June 24 at Menotomy (West Cambridge), Massachusetts, and concluded it by saying,

Live and act as Masons, that you may die as Masons; let those despisers see, alth' many of us cannot read, yet by our searches and researches into men and things, we have supplied that defect; and if they will let us we shall call ourselves a charter'd lodge of just and lawful Masons; be always ready to give an answer to those that ask you a question; give the right hand of affection and fellowship to whom it justly belongs; let their colour and complexion be what it will, let their nation be what it may, for they are your brethren, and it is your indispensable duty so to do; let them as Masons deny this, and we & the world know what to think of them be they ever so grand; for we know this was Solomon's creed, Solomon's creed did I say, it is the decree of the Almighty, and all Masons have learnt it.

This impassioned speech was subsequently endorsed by the Reverend William Bentley of Salem, Massachusetts, who later said of Hall that "he had no advantages, except such as he gained by his own diligence and his excellent moral habits." But Bentley, like all of Hall's admirers, was unable to help him establish a black school in Boston.

Finally, Hall took the matter into his own hands. In 1800, he recruited two students from Harvard University to serve as teachers for a school for blacks that he opened in his own home. Hall's school proved to be such a success that it had to be moved to a larger facility: the African Society House on Belknap Street. At the age of 65, Prince Hall could add the founding of Boston's first black school to his list of accomplishments. ⚭

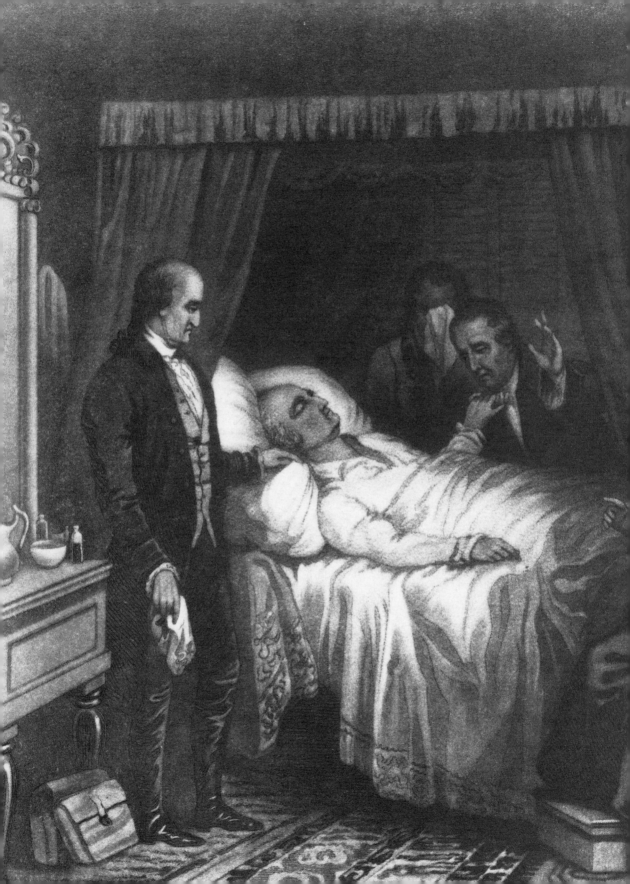

SERVING HIS PEOPLE

TWO MONTHS AFTER George Washington's death on December 13, 1799, Prince Hall's African Lodge members mourned the passing of their fellow Mason by walking through the streets of Boston in a solemn procession. Even though the first president of the United States had not shown himself to be a great friend of the black cause during the American Revolution, Hall and his fellow Masons were eager to indicate to the people of Boston that its black population was made up of loyal citizens.

Now in his mid-sixties, Hall himself was no longer a young man. Yet his health was still good enough for him to remain a forceful presence at the African Lodge, which met on the first Tuesday of each month. In addition, he could look back with pride at his many achievements, from founding the African Lodge and establishing a black school to petitioning for the betterment of blacks. What's more, he was an esteemed leather dresser, had fathered several children, and lived in what one government official termed "an elegant house."

Although President Washington had not been a great advocate of the black cause during the American Revolution, Hall and other black Masons mourned the death of their fellow Mason on December 13, 1799. Two months later, Hall helped honor Washington by walking through the streets of Boston in a solemn procession.

Nevertheless, Hall was not wholly satisfied with the world in which he lived. The plight of his race, which had always troubled him, grew even worse in 1800. That spring, two slaves, Gabriel Prosser and Jack Bowler, organized a massive rebellion against slave owners in Virginia. As Prosser began to stockpile weapons in preparation for the revolt, he told his recruits that he intended to spare only those whites who had opposed slavery.

On August 30, more than 1,000 of these rebel slaves gathered outside Richmond to begin their assault. The local militia had learned of the slaves' plans, however, and managed to crush the rebellion. Thirty-five of the slaves were executed, including Prosser.

Even though the revolt did not get very far, word of the rebellion spread across the country. Before long, there were rumors of slave revolts everywhere. "Let but a single armed Negro be seen or suspected," reported one Philadelphia newspaper, "and, at once, on many a lonely plantation, there were trembling hands at work to bar doors and windows that seldom had been even closed before, and there was shuddering when a grey squirrel scrambled over the roof, or a shower of walnuts came down clattering from the overhanging boughs."

A Boston newspaper responded to the Prosser rebellion by listing the names of more than 240 blacks who were "warned and directed to depart out of this commonwealth before the 10th day of October next, as they would avoid the pains and penalties of the law in that case provided." Try as they might, there was little Hall and other black leaders could say to convince whites that they should not fear blacks.

One of the ways Hall sought to quell the tensions between blacks and whites in Boston was by taking part in the Turtle Feast, an annual charity event held by the East Indian Marine Society. Hall served as the chief cook at the Turtle Feast on July 11, 1801, and clearly won the respect of the guests. Among the dishes he prepared was a giant pie served in a turtle shell.

Apparently, Hall was an excellent cook. According to one person who attended this charity event, "[A]s for a turtle feast, there was one outstanding expert: Prince Hall. A tall, lean Negro of great dignity, he always carried himself with the air of one who ruled many. Indeed he did, for whenever a well-to-do person wished the best catering job in eastern Massachusetts, he sent word to Prince Hall in Boston, and when the time came he appeared with a dozen of his black men, or two dozen, if the banquet was a large one."

Another person who attended the feast described Hall as "a person of great influence among his colour in great Boston, being Master of the African Lodge and a person to whom they refer with confidence their principal affairs. The Clergy were introduced to him and the principal gentlemen took notice of him. Brother Freeman of Boston pronounced him a very useful man and that the Masonic Negroes are evidently many grades above the common blacks of Boston."

Boston, however, was no longer the only city to boast an African Lodge. In 1797, a group of blacks established a lodge in Philadelphia. Hall promptly wrote to its founders: "We are willing to set you at work under our charter and Lodge No. 459 from London; under that authority and by the name of the African Lodge. We hereby and herein give you license to assemble and work as aforesaid under that denomination." Absalom Jones became Master of this lodge.

A small network of African lodges began to rise when a third lodge was founded, this time in Providence, Rhode Island. Hall took it upon himself to act

By the end of Hall's life, a small network of the black Masonic orders had begun to appear around the country. Hall provided charters for some and acted as provincial grand master of two other lodges.

as provincial grand master of these other two lodges, both of which promoted the Masonic values of benevolence and charity. The Masonic tradition would live on through Hall's followers.

Hall died in Boston on December 4, 1807, at the age of 72—his death certificate listing the cause of death as old age; his remains are said to be buried in St. Matthews Cemetery in Boston. In its eulogy of Hall, the African Grand Lodge called him "a useful citizen and soldier, a Christian minister, who discharged all his duties with a high order of intelligence. African Grand Lodge and the craft have been in mourning since."

Half a year after Hall's death, representatives from the Boston, Philadelphia, and Providence lodges held a meeting in which they voted to rename the African Lodge as the Prince Hall Lodge. Nearly 20 years later another major change was made to the lodge Prince Hall had founded. On June 26, 1827, the Prince Hall Lodge broke away from the Grand Lodge of England and declared itself "free and independent of any lodge from this day."

Today, Freemasonry is still segregated along racial lines, with white Masons refusing to acknowledge the legitimacy of the Prince Hall Lodge. Yet the Prince Hall Lodge continues to thrive. There are currently more than 5,000 lodges across the nation, with half a million members.

Many prominent blacks have become Prince Hall Masons, including the noted scholar and activist W. E. B. Du Bois and U.S. Supreme Court justice Thurgood Marshall. Like all black Masons, they have been counseled to follow Hall's example of working to uplift the community. Hall, for one, never lost sight of the reason why blacks should "live and act as Masons." As he told his African Lodge brethren at the end of his 1797 charge:

> Let blind admirers handsome faces praise,
> And graceful features to great honor raise,
> The glories of the red and white express,
> I know no beauty but in holiness;
> If God of beauty be the uncreate
> Perfect idea, in this lower state,
> The greatest beauties of an human mould
> Who most resemble Him we justly hold;
> Whom we resemble not in flesh and blood,
> But being pure and holy, just and good:
> May such a beauty fall but to my share,
> For curious shape or face I'll never care.

CHRONOLOGY

———— ❧ ————

1735   Prince Hall is born, probably in West Africa

1749   Becomes a slave of William Hall's in Boston

1756   Marries a slave named Delia; their son, Primus Hall, is born

1763   Hall marries Sara Ritchie; joins the Reverend Andrew Croswell's Congregational Church

1770   Manumitted by William Hall; marries Flora Gibbs; their son, Prince Africanus, is born

1775   Hall joins the Fraternal Order of the Free and Accepted Masons; organizes the African Lodge in Boston

1776   Enlists in the Continental army

1777   Sends an antislavery petition to the General Court of Massachusetts

1781   Declares the African Lodge's independence from the English Grand Lodge

1784   Refused by American lodges; applies to England for a charter for the African Lodge

1787   Receives the charter; sends to the General Court of Massachusetts a petition to allow blacks to return to Africa and a petition for equal education for blacks

1792   Delivers his first charge to his fellow black Masons

1796   Appeals to Boston officials for the establishment of a black school

1797   Delivers his second charge to his fellow black Masons; helps charter African lodges in Philadelphia and Providence

1800   Establishes the first black school in Boston

1807   Dies in Boston on December 4

FURTHER READING

Bennett, Lerone. *Before the Mayflower*. New York: Penguin Books, 1984.

Crawford, George. *Prince Hall and His Followers*. New York: AMS Press, 1971.

Franklin, John Hope. *From Slavery to Freedom: A History of Negro Americans*. New York: Knopf, 1980.

Green, Lorenzo J. *The Negro in Colonial New England*. New York: Atheneum, 1969.

Kaplan, Sidney. *The Black Presence in the Era of the American Revolution, 1770–1800*. Greenwich, CT: New York Graphic Society, 1973.

Klots, Steve. *Richard Allen*. New York: Chelsea House, 1991.

Langguth, A. J. *Patriots*. New York: Simon & Schuster, 1988.

Quarles, Benjamin. *The Negro in the American Revolution*. Chapel Hill: University of North Carolina Press, 1961.

Richmond, Merle. *Phillis Wheatley*. New York: Chelsea House, 1988.

Schouler, James. *Americans of 1776: Daily Life During the Revolutionary Period*. Williamstown, MA: Corner House, 1976.

Stevenson, David. *The Origins of Freemasonry*. Cambridge, England: Cambridge University Press, 1988.

Walkes, Joseph A., Jr. *Black Square and Compass: 200 Years of Prince Hall Freemasonry*. New York: Writers Press, 1979.

Wesley, Charles H. *Prince Hall: Life and Legacy*. Washington, DC: United Supreme Council, Southern Jurisdiction, Prince Hall Affiliation, 1983.

Williams, Loretta J. *Black Freemasonry and Middle Class Realities*. Columbia: University of Missouri Press, 1980.

INDEX

PICTURE CREDITS

ARTHUR DIAMOND was born in Queens, New York, and has lived and worked in Colorado, New Mexico, and Oregon. He holds a bachelor's degree in English from the University of Oregon and a master's degree in English/Writing from Queens College. A former book editor in New York City, he now writes full-time and is the author of several nonfiction books, including *Paul Cuffe* in the BLACK AMERICANS OF ACHIEVEMENT series published by Chelsea House. He currently lives in Queens with his wife, Irina, and their son, Benjamin Thomas.

NATHAN IRVIN HUGGINS is W.E.B. Du Bois Professor of History and Director of the W.E.B. Du Bois Institute for Afro-American Research at Harvard University. He previously taught at Columbia University. Professor Huggins is the author of numerous books, including *Black Odyssey: The Afro-American Ordeal in Slavery*, *The Harlem Renaissance*, and *Slave and Citizen: The Life of Frederick Douglass*.